STONE AGE GEOMETRY
TRIANGLES

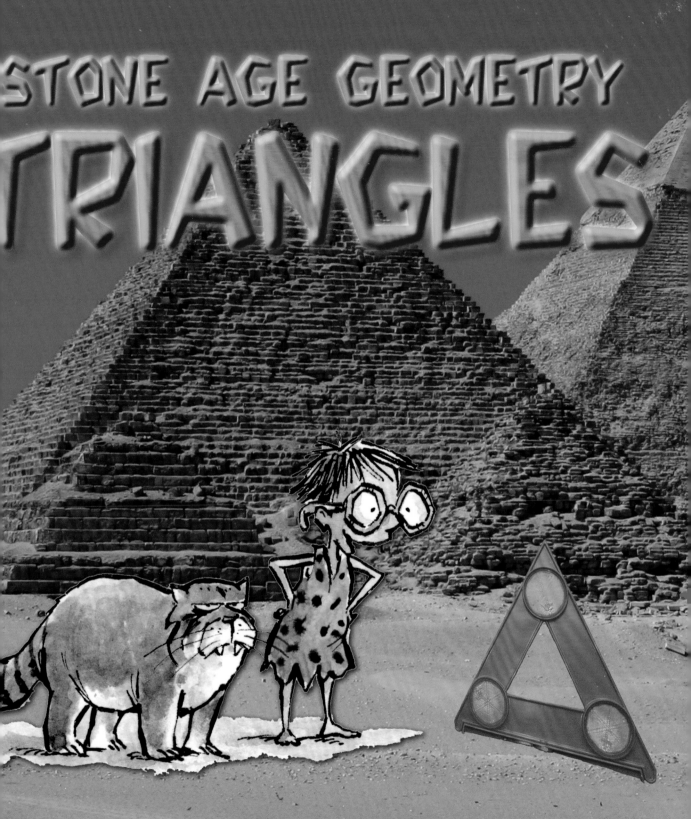

Gerry Bailey & Felicia Law
Illustrated by
Mike Phillips

 Crabtree Publishing Company
www.crabtreebooks.com
1-800-387-7650

Published in Canada	**Published in the United States**
616 Welland Ave.	PMB 59051, 350 Fifth Ave.
St. Catharines, ON	59th Floor,
L2M 5V6	New York, NY 10118

Published in **2014 by CRABTREE PUBLISHING COMPANY.** All rights reserved. No part of this publication may be reproduced, stored in a retrieval system, or transmitted in any form or by any means, electronic, mechanical, photocopy, recording or otherwise, without the prior written permission of the copyright owner.

Printed in Canada/032014/MA20140124

Authors: Gerry Bailey & Felicia Law
Illustrator: Mike Phillips
Editor: Kathy Middleton
Proofreader: Anastasia Suen
End matter: Kylie Korneluk
**Production coordinator and
   Prepress technician:** Samara Parent
Print coordinator: Margaret Amy Salter

Copyright © 2012 BrambleKids Ltd.

Photographs:
Cover - EcOasis (r) risteski goce Title Page – Main image EcOasis (r) risteski goce Pg 2 – Gerald Lacz, age footstock/superstock Pg 3 –David M. Schrader Pg 5 – (t) Costin Cojocaru (m) anaken2012 (b) Vadi Kozlovsky Pg 7 – (t) Marc Dietrich (m) Benedictus (b) Guapsi Pg 9 – (t) olly (b) Lukiyanova Natalia/frenta Pg 11 – (bl) Tony Froyen (br) woodsy (tr) Stephen Aaron Rees Pg 13 - ((bl) twobee (br) Heiko Kiera (tl) Yuriy Boyko (tr) hansenn Pg 14 - spirit of america Pg 14/15 (tc) Pierre Jacques/Hemis/Corbi Pg 15 – (l) Bobkeenan Photography (r) Giancarlo Liguori (br) spirit of america Pg 21 – (t) basel10165 (r) Pete Pahham (b) Carl Staub Pg 23 – (t) Mikel Martinez (b) Matteo Festi Pg 25 – (t) spirit of america (br) Dan Breckwoldt Pg 27 – (t) Bjorn Stefanson (b) Steve Newton Pg 29 – (tl) visceralimage (br) LeDo (r) Tony Linck / SuperStock Pg 31 – (tl) Yaroslav (tm) Yaroslav (tr) DEKANARYAS (b) StudioSmart

All images are shutterstock unless otherwise stated

Library and Archives Canada Cataloguing in Publication

Bailey, Gerry, author
     Stone age geometry: Triangles / Gerry Bailey, Felicia Law ; illustrator: Mike Phillips.

(Stone age geometry)
Includes index.
Issued in print and electronic formats.
ISBN 978-0-7787-0512-3 (bound).--ISBN 978-0-7787-0518-5 (pbk.).--ISBN 978-1-4271-8237-1 (html).--ISBN 978-1-4271-9007-9 (pdf)

     1. Triangle--Juvenile literature. 2. Geometry--Juvenile literature.
I. Law, Felicia, author II. Phillips, Mike, 1961-, illustrator III. Title.

QA482.B352 2014   j516'.154   C2014-900428-1
                                                         C2014-900429-X

Library of Congress Cataloging-in-Publication Data

Bailey, Gerry, author.
Stone age geometry : Triangles / Gerry Bailey & Felicia Law ; illustrated by M Phillips.
     pages cm. -- (Stone age geometry)
Includes index.
 ISBN 978-0-7787-0512-3 (reinforced library binding : alk. paper) -- ISBN 978-0-7787-0518-5 (pbk. : alk. paper) -- ISBN 978-1-4271-8237-1 (electroni html : alk. paper) -- ISBN 978-1-4271-9007-9 (electronic pdf : alk. paper)
1. Triangle--Juvenile literature. 2. Geometry--Juvenile literature.
I. Law, Felicia, author. II. Phillips, Mike, 1961- illustrator. III. Title.

QA482.B344 2014
516.154--dc23
                                                     2014002074

LEO'S LESSONS:

MEET LEO

Meet Leo, Brightest kid on the block.

So that's Leo!

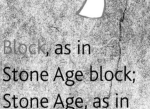

Bright, as in IQ off the scale; inventive, as in Leonardo da Vinci inventive; and way, way ahead of his time....

Block, as in Stone Age block; Stone Age, as in 30,000 years ago.

Then there's Pallas— Leo's pet.

Pallas is wild, and he's OK with being called Stone Age too; after all, his ancestors have been around for millions of years. That's more than you can say for Leo's! You won't see many Pallas cats around today, unless you happen to be visiting the icy, cold wasteland of Arctic Siberia (at the top of Russia).

THREE SIDES

"Help me!" says Leo. He is holding a long branch in his hands. "I'm building a landing pad."

"What's a landing pad?" asks Pallas, scratching his ea

"It's a place where things land," answers Leo, "and it has to be in this shape."

"See?" says Leo. "It's a shape made with three sides called a triangle."

Pallas helps Leo set out the triangle using long branches.

"Awesome," says Leo. "Now all we have to do is wait for them to land."

"Them?" asks Pallas.

"The geese," says Leo. "Look!"

And Pallas looks up. He sees the geese flying down toward them in a perfect V-shape.

TRIANGLE

A triangle is a three-sided shape. The sides don't have to be the same length.

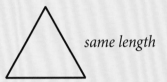

same length

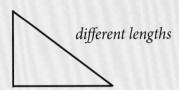

different lengths

The size and shape of a corner where two lines meet is called an angle. A triangle has three angles.

The size of an angle is measured in degrees, which is written with this sign °. In some triangles, all three angles are the same size. In other triangles, the angles are different sizes.

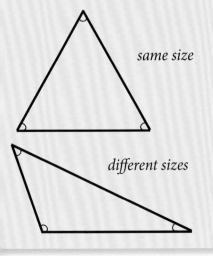

same size

different sizes

V-SHAPED FLIGHT

Many birds fly in a triangle shape when they **migrate** long distances in flocks. This helps them save energy by using the upwash, or upward movement of air, created by the wings of the birds in front. The triangle shape also helps the flock communicate with one another and find direction.

Origami is the art of folding paper at different angles.

This piece of art uses triangles of different sizes.

THE TRIANGLE FAMILY

"We're going camping," says Leo. "We'll sleep under the stars for two nights."

"Under the stars?" says Pallas. "You mean we sleep on the grass covered with creepy-crawlies and sniffed at by wild animals?"

"No," says Leo. "We'll have a tent. We'll use these skins and stretch them over a frame of sticks. See? A teepee—it's a perfect triangle, and so is the doorway."

Pallas makes his own teepee.

He doesn't find
it easy at all!

KINDS OF TRIANGLES

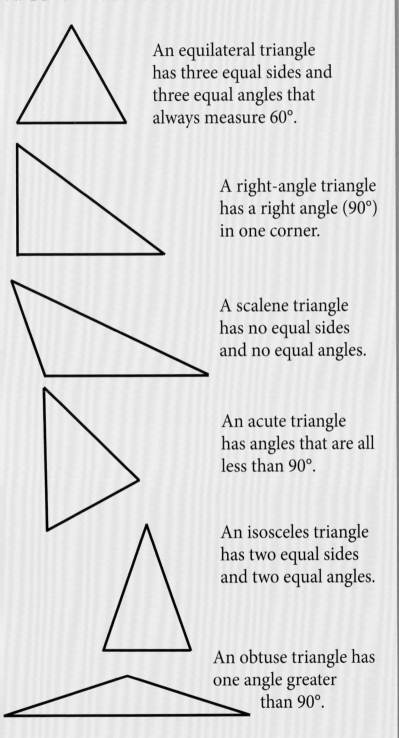

An equilateral triangle has three equal sides and three equal angles that always measure 60°.

A right-angle triangle has a right angle (90°) in one corner.

A scalene triangle has no equal sides and no equal angles.

An acute triangle has angles that are all less than 90°.

An isosceles triangle has two equal sides and two equal angles.

An obtuse triangle has one angle greater than 90°.

At the start of a **billiard game**, the balls are set up in a frame the shape of an equilateral triangle.

This teepee also forms a perfect equilateral triangle.

This playground slide forms the shape of a scalene triangle.

7

ANGLES

Leo is busy again. He is building a tower.
When it is finished, he will climb to the top
and use it as a lookout.

"What will you look out for?" asks Pallas.

"Dangerous animals," says Leo. "Big, hairy
mammoths, cave bears, and saber-tooth tigers—your
buddies with sharp claws and hungry stomachs."

"I need a lookout too," says Pallas. "I need to watch for
hunters—YOUR buddies with sharp spears and hungry
stomachs."

"OK, OK," says Leo. "You can climb up too."

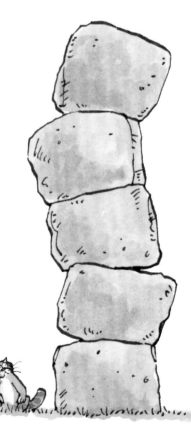

Pallas looks at the tower. It isn't very tall, but it
is already leaning over at a dangerous angle.

"Don't worry," says Leo. "I'm going to straighten
it up."

Leo builds the tower higher and higher.
But somehow it never looks very straight!

ANGLES

All triangles have three sides that meet at corners. The point where lines meet is called a vertex. The size and shape of a corner is measured as a kind of angle.

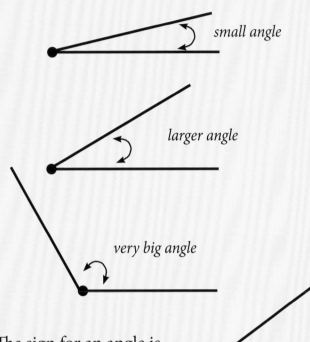

small angle

larger angle

very big angle

The sign for an angle is a small curve between the sides that join to make the angle.

The three angles of a triangle always add up to 180 degrees (180°).

*The legs of this **telescope** form a triangle with the ground. The three angles that are created add up to 180 degrees.*

The famous Leaning Tower of Pisa tilts at an angle of just under 4°.

"OK!" says Leo. "This way!"

"Where are we going," says Pallas.
"No, just you!" says Leo. "You have to follow the trail.
See? I laid a trail of leaves for you to follow through
the forest. It's a challenge to see if you get lost
or not."

"Of course I'll get lost," says Pallas.

"No you won't. All the leaves are arrow-shaped.
They are triangles, and they point in the
right direction."

Pallas sets off. He follows the arrows that point a
path through the forest. He is back in ten minutes.

"Easy!" he says.

Leo is impressed. He had turned some of the leaves
the wrong way to trick Pallas. But the trick hadn't
worked. So how had Pallas found the right path?

"Well," says Pallas. "I'm a cat. I didn't bother with the
arrows. I just followed your smell."

EQUILATERAL TRIANGLE

A triangle that has all three sides the same length is called an equilateral triangle.

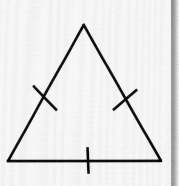

To show that the sides of an equilateral triangle have equal lengths, you put a short line across the middle of each side.

If a triangle has three sides of equal length, the angles will be equal too. The angles will all be 60°.

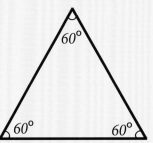

To show that the angles are the same you put identical curves on each angle.

Equilateral triangles make good signs. These two say it's okay to ride a bike or a horse on a trail.

Mathieu Heamekers, the Dutch artist and mathematician, created this triangle sculpture which stands in the center of the village of Ophoven, Belgium.

A brightly colored equilateral triangle is used as a warning sign on the highway.

11

ISOSCELES TRIANGLES

Leo is tidying the cave.
"This goes here," he mutters. "That goes there."

"Move!" he tells Pallas. "I'm going to hang these
skins up so they don't get so creased."

"But this is my bed," says Pallas.
"No," says Leo. "It's not YOUR bed. It's MY pile of clothes,
and look how crumpled you've made them!"

Leo takes three short sticks. He binds them together in a triangle.
He twists a hook into the point at the top and holds it up for
Pallas to see.
"See," he says, "a coat hanger."

But Pallas isn't interested. He doesn't need a coat hanger.
He needs a bed!

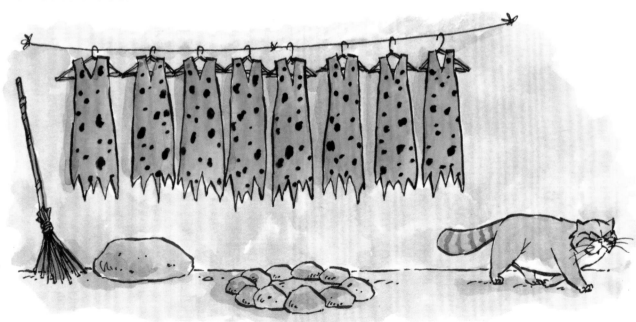

ISOSCELES TRIANGLE

An isosceles triangle has two equal sides. The two angles opposite the equal sides are also equal. Usually the side of the triangle that has a different length is called the base.

An isosceles triangle can have a longer base than its two sides.

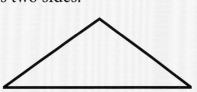

It can also have a shorter base.

A coat hanger is an isosceles triangle with a longer base than its sides.

These flags are in the shape of isosceles triangles. Their base is shorter than the two sides.

When you stand far enough back to look, you can see these trees are in the shape of an isosceles triangle.

The shell of this armadillo is covered in markings shaped like isosceles triangles.

13

BUILDING WITH TRIANGLES

Triangles are used to build things because they provide great strength. You can see triangular shapes in churches and bridges and homes. In construction, a triangular-shaped frame is known as a truss. A triangular-shaped part of the roof is called a gable.

A triangle is a strong shape for building because the forces on a triangle are distributed evenly along its three sides. A triangle will keep its shape because any two sides support the third side. This support keeps the structure from collapsing.

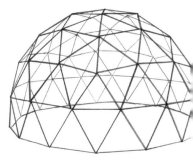

Triangles can be fitted together to form a shape called a geodesic dome. The geodesic dome is a kind of truss.

The Millau Viaduct in southern France
is called a cable-stayed bridge. The cables
that support the road are arranged in a
triangle shape from each **mast**.

A gable is a triangular section that
sticks up from the roof of a building.

Triangles were used to
build the Eiffel Tower
in Paris, France, to
make it strong.

15

SCALENE TRIANGLES

"What are you doing?" asks Leo.
"I'm fixing my bike," says Pallas. "The frame is not strong enough."

"It's not just the frame," says Leo.
"The whole thing is wonky. Your bike is falling to pieces!
It would be quicker to start again."

Pallas picks up the pieces one by one.
Leo's right. It might be easier to just start again!

They find five sturdy bars for the new frame.
This one won't fall to pieces.
The saddle, the handlebars, the pedals, the
gears, and the wheels all fit into place.

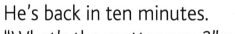

Pallas climbs on and pedals away.

He's back in ten minutes.
"What's the matter now?" asks Leo.

Pallas explains.

The members of SACC—the Stone Age
Cycle Club—all want a new bike like
his. They all want a new frame that's
sturdy and won't fall to pieces.

SCALENE TRIANGLE

A scalene triangle has no equal sides. It also has no equal-size angles. Tick marks across each side show equal or non-equal side lengths. A scalene triangle has one, two, and three tick marks to show each side is a different length.

This tool, called a set square or triangle, is used to measure angles. Its shape is an isosceles triangle.

Can you see the two triangles that makes up the frame of this bicycle? It's usually called a diamond frame.

17

RIGHT-ANGLE TRIANGLES

"Hey!" says Pallas. "There's two of you.
One up there and one down here."

"That's my shadow," says Leo.
"It's not the real ME."

"Well it's real enough," says Pallas.
"It goes everywhere you go,
and it copies all your actions."

Leo stands up straight.
Pallas is right.
His shadow stretches out
in front of him in a tall line.

It makes a perfect, right-angled corner at his feet.

"You've got a shadow, too, " says Leo.
But no matter how Pallas stands,
his shadow is always a round blob!

RIGHT-ANGLE TRIANGLE

A right-angle triangle has one angle that measures 90°. A 90° angle is called a right angle. It is marked inside the angle with a square.

The line opposite the 90° angle is called the hypotenuse. It's the longest side of the triangle. The other two sides are called the "legs."

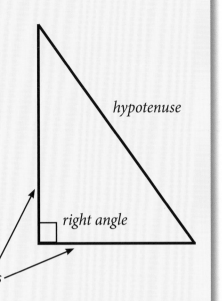

hypotenuse

right angle

legs

The sails of a yacht are in the shape of right-angle triangles.

When the sun is out, your shadow falls on the ground at a right angle to your body.

Sundials

The sundial was one of the first tools people used to measure the time of day. It is usually made from a stone pillar that had a flat, round top. A pointer, called a gnomon, is attached to the top. The pointer is shaped like a slanted triangle.

A time scale, marked in hours, is drawn around the edge of the sundial. The shadow cast from the gnomon falls on the hour scale telling what hour of the day it is.

The shadow falls at 90° and points to the correct time.

You can make a simple sundial by drawing a clock face round a stick.

19

MUSICAL TRIANGLES

"We need a new instrument for the band,"
says Leo.
"Band?" says Pallas. "There are only two of us!"

"I know," says Leo. "That's why we need more
instruments. We need to make more sound."

"I can bang on the drums a bit harder,"
says Pallas.
"And I could blow on the mammoth tusk
in time to the beat."

"It's not noise we need, Pallas," says Leo.
"It's music!"

Leo gets to work making a new instrument.
He joins three bird bones together to make a
triangle. When he hits it with a stick, the hollow
bones echo and play a note.

Then he makes triangles of different sizes
that each play a different note.

"OK," says Pallas. "Can I sing along?"
"If you must!" says Leo.

And Pallas sings:
"Cool cats catch fool rats, yeah, yeah, yeah!"

The balalaika is a Russian stringed instrument shaped like a triangle. It has a three-sided body, made mostly of wood. A balalaika has three strings.

The triangle is played like this.

Triangles make music

The triangle is a **percussion** instrument. It is usually made of steel, but other metals such as copper can be used. The triangle dangles from a thread or wire and is hit with a bar.

The bar, called a striker, is also made of metal to give the sound a ringing tone. Nothing else can touch the triangle as it is played or it would stop the vibrations that make the sound.

Keller Williams, an American musician, often uses percussion instruments in his jazz and rock music.

Composers began using triangles in their music during the 1700s. Famous composers such as Mozart, Haydn, and Beethoven all used triangles in their music. But it was Franz Liszt who first used it as a solo instrument in his Piano Concerto No. 1.

Today, even rock bands sometimes use a triangle.

RAMPS

Pallas is in training.
It's the Mutts Cat Show in a week,
and he is entered in the **Agility** Competition.

"The trouble," says Leo, "is that you're not very agile.
I mean, you don't run very fast. You can't jump very high.
And you get out of breath when you have to climb hills."

But Pallas wants to try.

He squeezes in and out of the bars, but then he
gets stuck. It takes lots of pushing to set him fre

He jumps over the hurdle, but he knocks it dowr
It takes lots of rebuilding to set it back up.

He runs up the ramp, but he can't run down.

"Why not?" asks Leo.
"I don't like slopes," says Pallas.
"I might slip and fall."

Pallas sits at the top of
the ramp. There's no way he
can think of to get down...

...except to slide on
his bottom.

OBTUSE TRIANGLE

An obtuse triangle is a triangle that has at least one obtuse angle. An obtuse angle is a wide angle that is between 90 degrees and 180 degrees.

The longest side of the triangle is always opposite the obtuse angle.

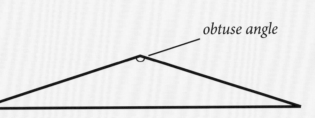

obtuse angle

In this triangle, the obtuse angle is the one opposite the base.

The roof of this building spreads in a wide obtuse angle. If you drew a line from one edge of the roof to the other, it would create an obtuse triangle.

The dog is climbing a ramp that has an obtuse angle at the top. The angle is more than 90 degrees and less than 180 degrees.

23

A PYRAMID

"Wow, what's that?" asks Pallas. "It's really high."

Leo and Pallas gaze at the pile of stones.
The stones are piled in layers like steps,
rising to a point at the top.

"It's a pyramid of some kind," says Leo.
"That's what this shape is called."
"But why put a pile of stones here?"
says Pallas.

"It's a burial place," says Leo, "there are
dead people—bones and stuff—under it."
"In that case," says Pallas, "you can go up
on your own!"

"There'll be a great view from the top," says Leo.
"You can tell me all about it when you come down,"
says Pallas. So Leo sets off alone.

Pallas sits and waits. He sniffs the air.
There's a strong smell of bones. Pallas can smell
a bone anywhere. These smell like old bones
to Pallas, but they're still bones.

Pallas starts to scratch, He starts to dig.
He scratches and digs, and he finds bones.

Very old bones!

24

PYRAMID

A pyramid is a structure with three or four triangle-shaped sides. The base of the pyramid can be a triangle or a square.

The point at the top where the four sides meet is called the apex.

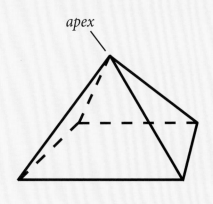

apex

The Louvre Pyramid is a large glass and metal pyramid. It stands in the main courtyard of the famous museum in the Louvre Palace in Paris, France.

Ancient pyramids

The **Maya** people of Central America built pyramids as high as a twenty-story building. These are called step pyramids because each layer forms a step leading up to the **temple** at the top.

The pyramids at Giza in Egypt were built over 4,000 years ago as tombs to hold the mummies and belongings of kings called pharaohs. These enormous stone structures required hundreds of thousands of workers to build them.

PENTAGONS

Leo tells Pallas to stand very still.

He draws a shape around Pallas,
marking it in the ground.
"It's a magic shape," he says.

It doesn't look very magical to Pallas.
It's an ordinary kind of shape with five sides,
all the same length.

"It's a pentagon shape," says Leo. "And now I am
going to do some magic."

Pallas isn't worried.
"What kind of magic?" he says.

"Stand very still," says Leo, "while I say the magic
word. Abracadabra!"

Leo waits. Pallas waits. Nothing happens.

"Oh dear!" sighs Leo. "You were supposed to turn
into a rabbit."

"Don't be ridiculous," says Pallas, walking away.
But suddenly he wonders what carrots taste like.

PENTAGON

A pentagon is a five-sided polygon, which is a flat shape with three or more straight sides. All the lines of a pentagon connect. The sides and angles can be different from one other. But if all the sides and angles are equal, it's called a regular pentagon.

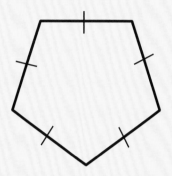

The angles of a regular pentagon each measure 108 degrees.

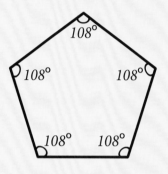

Home plate in baseball is shaped like a pentagon.

The Pentagon

The Pentagon is a building in Arlington County, Virginia, that is the headquarters of the United States Department of Defense. The building gets its name from its shape. Around 26,000 military and other people work there.

The building's five pentagon-shaped rings-within-rings can be seen when viewed from above.

A soccer ball is made of pentagon shapes sewn together.

HEXAGONS

Leo is looking very odd.
He seems to have some kind of helmet on his head.
"Put this on," he tells Pallas. "It will protect your head."

"What from?" asks Pallas.
"Why do I need to protect
my head?"

"From the bees," says Leo.
"We're going to collect the honey."

Leo explains how it's done.

First he lights something called a smoker.
"Smoke calms the bees," he tells Pallas.

Then he opens the hive and removes the frames.

He takes out one frame of honey at a time,
carefully brushing off any dozy bees.

The honeycombs in the frames are formed from
hundreds of perfectly-shaped hexagons.
Each hexagon is filled with golden honey.
Leo scrapes off his honey into a pot.

Pallas doesn't need a pot. He just dips his paw in.
Cats don't need manners.

HEXAGON

A hexagon is a six-sided polygon. It gets its name from the Greek word *hex*, which means six.

It has six sides and six corners, or vertices.

When all six sides are equal, it's called a regular hexagon.

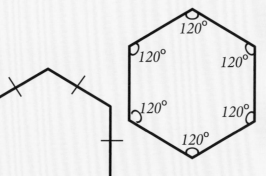

Each angle in a regular hexagon is 120 degrees.

A regular hexagon can be divided into six equilateral triangles.

Snowflakes occur in hexagonal patterns.

The pieces of a turtle shell, known as scutes, are hexagon-shaped.

Bees construct their honeycombs in a hexagonal pattern. Hexagon-shaped honeycombs are very efficient. They don't need a lot of wax to construct and keep their shape when squeezed up to each other.

PRISMS

"Look at that," says Pallas, pointing to the sky.

"It's a rainbow," says Leo. "Light is bouncing off the raindrops in the air and breaking into all its different colors.

Look, you can see from red all the way through to violet. There are six colors altogether. When you see them in a band like that it is called a spectrum."

Pallas wants to see the colors close up so Leo shows him how.

"Here's that triangular piece of glass we found in the volcano," he says. "It's all polished and smooth. It will act like a prism and break the light.

"Now watch," he tells Pallas, and he holds up the prism to the sunlight.

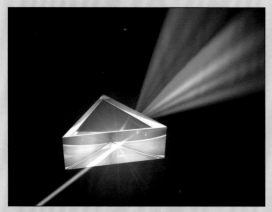

A prism bends light to break it into its different colors.

A prism

A prism is a triangular-shaped block of glass that can be used to break up sunlight, called white light. White light is actually made up of a mixture of colors. When light hits the side of a prism, its colors bend, or change their path. Different colors bend at different angles, so when they come out of the other side of the prism, we see them as something like a rainbow.

LEARNING MORE

OTHER BOOKS

Basher Science: Algebra and Geometry
by Dan Green and Simon Basher
Kingfisher (2011).

Mummy Math: An Adventure in Geometry
by Cindy Neuschwander, illustrated by Bryan Langdo.
Square Fish (2009).

The Greedy Triangle
By Marilyn Burns, illustrated by Gordon Silveria
Scholastic Paperbacks (2008).

WEBSITES

Get the facts on the triangle and its properties at these entertaining websites:

www.ducksters.com/kidsmath/triangles.php

www.coolmath.com/reference/triangles-types.html

Find a variety of games and activities with geometry themes.

www.kidsmathgamesonline.com/geometry.html

This website provides information on shapes and their properties.

www.mathsisfun.com/geometry/index.html

KEY WORDS

An apex is the pointed top of a shape, object or building, where the sides meet.

The base is the longest side of a triangle facing the other two sides which are of shorter length.

The hypotenuse is the longest side of a right-angle triangle.

A truss is used in architecture. It is a structure made up of one or more triangular units connected by joints and is used to help hold up beams or a roof.

A vertex is a corner point of a triangle where two of its lines meet. The plural of vertex is vertices.

GLOSSARY

agility Able to move quickly and easily

billiard game A game played with a cue stick which is used to strike billiard balls, moving them around a cloth-covered table

mast An upright tall pole

Maya A member of a group of Indian peoples of the Yucatán Peninsula and neighboring areas

migrate To move from one region or climate to another usually for feeding or breeding

percussion The act of tapping sharply

telescope A tubular tool used for viewing distant objects (as objects in outer space) by focusing light rays with mirrors or lenses

temple A building for worship

INDEX